# THE ROLLING STONES

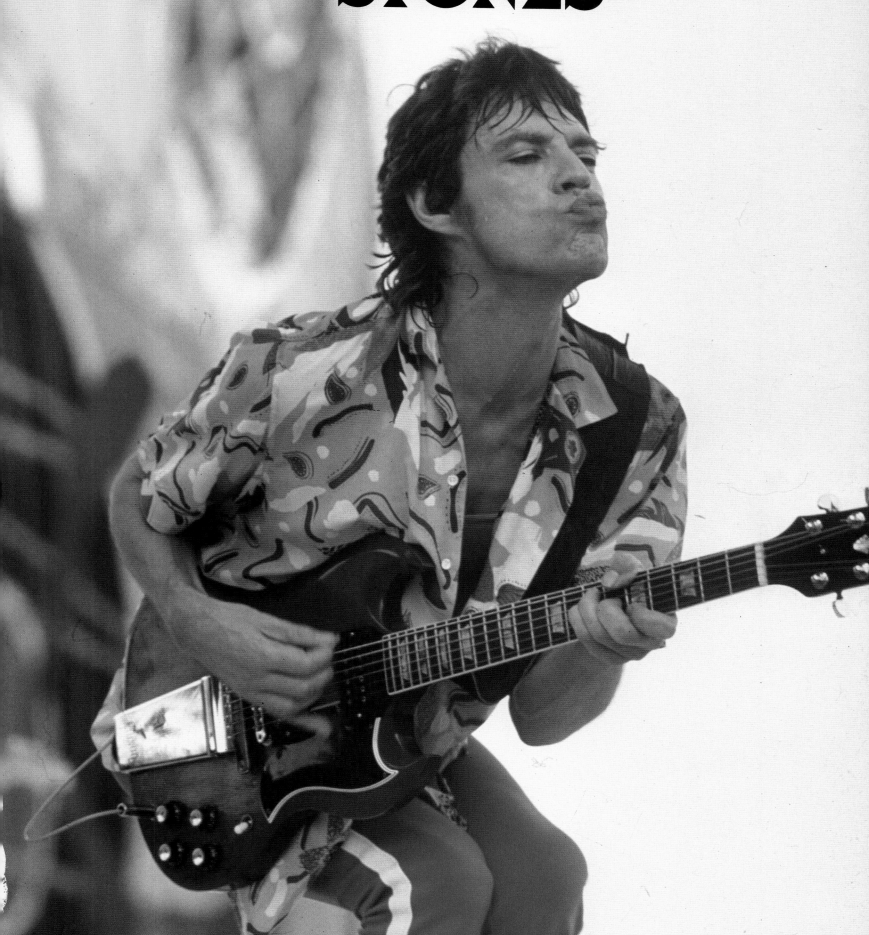

# THE ROLLING STONES

## William Ruhlmann

SMITHMARK

This edition published in 1993
by SMITHMARK Publishers Inc.,
16 East 32nd Street
New York, New York 10016.

SMITHMARK books are available for bulk purchase for sales promotion and premium use. For details write or telephone the Manager of Special Sales, SMITHMARK Publishers Inc., 16 East 32nd Street, New York, NY 10016. (212) 532-6600.

Produced by Brompton Books Corp.,
15 Sherwood Place,
Greenwich, CT 06830.

ISBN 0-8317-7367-7

Printed in Hong Kong

10 9 8 7 6 5 4 3 2 1

*Page 1:* One of rock and roll's greatest performers, Mick Jagger is famous for being able to both shock and charm his audience.

*Previous pages:* Mick Jagger struts his stuff before a full house during the 1982 tour.

*These pages:* 'Respectable:' The Rolling Stones (l-r) Charlie Watts, Keith Richards, Mick Jagger, Ron Wood, Bill Wyman.

**PICTURE CREDITS**

AP/Wide World: 17(bottom).
Brompton Photo Library: 6(both), 7, 8, 9(both), 11, 16(top), 19, 22, 26(bottom), 29, 39, 42(bottom), 56(both), 62-63(all three), 65, 66-67(all three), 72-73(right), 79, 84, 88.
Claude Gassian: 40, 44(left), 45(right), 48-49, 50-51(all four), 53, 54, 55, 68, 69, 80-81, 82(top), 83, 86-87, 91.
Globe Photos: 8-9(center), 10(right), 18, 24-25, 27, 32, 35, 38(bottom), 64; Alpha: 85; David Bailey: 36(left); John Barrett: 74(top), Fred Bauman: 30(bottom); Cecil Beaton/Camera Press: 33(top); Dave Benett: 75; Richard Corken: 59; Michael Ferguson: 90; Sylvia Norris: 21; Rangefinders: 72; Scanfoto: 82(top); Adam Scull: 70(left); Tom Smith: 20; Wendy Workman: 74(bottom); Zitwer: 43.
Photo Features/Relay: 41(right); A. Byrne: 41(left); Andre Csillag: 58(bottom), 70-71(bottom); Chalk Davies: 57; David Wainwright: 60-61.
Retna: 44-45(center); King Collection: 12, 13(both), 14-15(all three), 23(both); Lawrence Kirsch: 1; Michael Putland: 2-3, 4-5, 46-47(all three).
Reuters/Bettmann: 78(both).
UPI/Bettmann Newsphotos: 10(left), 26(top), 28(both), 30-31(top), 33(bottom), 34, 37(top right, bottom right), 38(top), 76-77.
Fred and Beth Weiler: 16(bottom), 17(top).

# *Contents*

# *Introduction*

In popular music, two years at the top is about the most an entertainer can hope for. If persistent, and if accompanied by a modicum of luck, a pop music performer can sustain a professional career and a reasonable income for much longer, of course. But the upper reaches – the Number One hits, the million sellers, the sold-out tours, the magazine covers, and the fan adulation – tend to come, if they come at all, in a rush, as one, inexplicably, catches the fancy of the public. At that moment, all is success and attention and hurry. But then, with that next record, that next look, that next concert tour, the moment has passed. There may be more hits, but they won't be as big, and the crowds and the press interest – and the paychecks – will also diminish. Then the identification one has achieved with the heady success of before, that signature song, becomes simultaneously a millstone and a meal ticket. You'd better like that hit – you'll be singing it every night for a long time to come.

This common scenario might have been as true for the Rolling Stones as it has been for hundreds of other stars. From the time that the Stones solidified their

lineup in January 1963 to their first American Number One hit, '(I Can't Get No) Satisfaction,' in July 1965, the group rose steadily in popularity, gradually outstripping all the British Invasion rock stars who followed the Beatles until they were second only to the Beatles themselves.

There followed the standard two years of fame, 1965-1967, during which the Stones consistently hit the Top Ten with their singles and albums, while their concert tours were riots of teen enthusiasm. But by the

*Left:* Keith Richards and Mick Jagger, the 'Glimmer Twins,' who have led the Rolling Stones since the mid-1960s.

*Above:* Ill-fated guitarist Brian Jones, the Stones' original leader.

*Right:* The original lineup of the Rolling Stones (left to right) Charlie Watts, Mick Jagger, Bill Wyman, Keith Richards, and Brian Jones, at the height of their initial fame in the mid-1960s.

fall of 1967, when their 15th American single, 'Dande-lion,' broke a string of nine straight Top Ten hits by peaking at Number 14; when they were bedeviled by drug convictions that threatened their freedom and re-stricted their ability to tour; when they broke with the manager/producer who had guided them to success; and when they found themselves negotiating their way uncertainly in a changing pop music trend moving away from their blues rock roots, it would have been easy to predict that the Rolling Stones' days at the top were numbered. In fact, they didn't even seem likely to be in the business much longer.

But instead of fading, the Stones stormed back. Abandoning their psychedelic experiments of 1967, they returned to a hard rock sound with their 1968 single 'Jumpin' Jack Flash,' coincidentally just as pop music itself returned to a more basic approach and the blues revival of the late 1960s kicked in. More import-ant, the Stones sorted out their problems and carried on, even at the cost of jettisoning guitarist Brian Jones, the man who gave the band its name. By the fall of 1969, when they returned to the concert circuit in triumph, the Stones were bigger than ever.

Like Frank Sinatra, one of the few pop stars who can challenge their longevity, who survived a career slump in the early 1950s to dominate his style of music from then on, the Stones never looked back after that pause. That's not to suggest that their career was smooth sail-ing in the 1970s, 1980s, and 1990s. In fact, they may have had the most turbulent history of any rock band ever. But with the second wind they found in the late 1960s, the Stones broke through the conventions of show business to achieve an unassailable status that they then went on to maintain ever after.

It's fair to say that just as they benefited from the re-turn of pop style to simple rock in the late 1960s, so they benefited in a more general way from the dominance rock was able to maintain in popular music from the mid-1960s onward. Sinatra may have been the king of the pop singers, but you can only be so big when the style of music you perform has itself passed from the main stage. The Stones have been fortunate that their chosen genre, blues-based rock 'n' roll, has turned out to be the longest-lasting musical trend of the century. Mitch Miller may have called it a passing fad, but, going on 40 years later, rock 'n' roll hasn't passed yet.

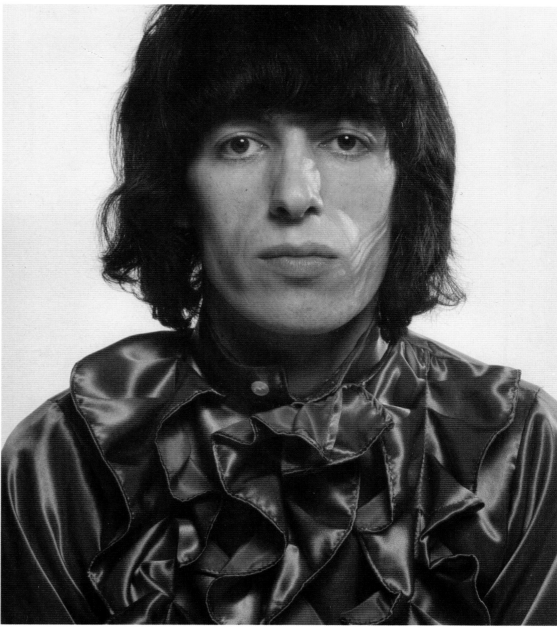

*Top left:* Drummer Charlie Watts makes a fashion statement, circa 1967.

*Above:* Mick Taylor replaced Brian Jones in 1969 and quit the Stones in 1974.

*Top right:* Bassist Bill Wyman in a frilly Carnaby Street number, circa 1967.

*Right:* Ron Wood (shown onstage during the 1981 American tour) joined the Stones provisionally in 1975, and permanently in 1976.

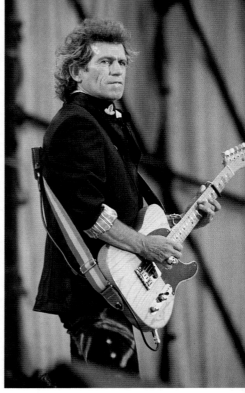

*Left:* Mick Jagger emotes during the opening night of the Stones' Steel Wheels tour in Philadelphia, August 31, 1989, their first performance together in seven years.

*Above:* Keith Richards onstage during the Stones' Steel Wheels/Urban Jungle tour, 1989-90.

*Top right:* Charlie Watts, Mick Jagger, and Keith Richards rock during the Stones' 1981 American tour.

Of course, it isn't just extraordinary good fortune that has kept the Rolling Stones in the pop forefront all this time. Part of what makes rock 'n' roll itself exciting is the balance it maintains between rigid control and chaos. Anchored to a relentless beat, the music nevertheless goes off on unexpected tangents, with noisy guitars slashing across melodies and shouted lyrics accentuating the harshness of the sound.

Musically, the Stones (whose name, even if borrowed from a Muddy Waters blues tune, literally means rock 'n' roll) are experts at expressing that tension. Drummer Charlie Watts brings a light, jazz-influenced touch to his playing that imbues his beat with a hint of swing. But he never overplays and never solos, and that's deliberate. The function of drumming, he once told the author, 'is to keep time.'

The function of guitar playing, Keith Richards might reply, is to construct a noisy, rhythmic sound field in which chords clash and bent strings vibrate strangely in a near-cacophony that nevertheless maintains momentum and coherence. And somewhere in the middle is Mick Jagger, whose personality cannot be divorced from his voice, posturing, slurring, and phrasing as though he only barely cares what the actual lyrics of the song (which he probably wrote) are, so long as he can use them as a vehicle to draw attention to himself.

As such, the Stones are the quintessential rock 'n' roll band. But their music is reflected in their lives. That solid, steady drummer has a solid, steady domestic life including a marriage that's lasted since 1964. The

guitarist who risks musical mayhem also has risked his life with a drug addiction that threatened to derail the band. And that posturing singer has become one of the most famous names and faces of the post-WWII era.

Somehow, such apparently volatile elements (mixed with replacement guitarist Ron Wood and former band members Ian Stewart, Brian Jones, Mick Taylor, and Bill Wyman) have not only coalesced into one of the most successful pop music acts of the century, but also have stayed together as their peers have come and gone and remained massively popular despite the ever-changing pop audience and its musical whims.

Nineteen ninety-three is the year that Mick Jagger and Keith Richards turn 50. Charlie Watts turns 52. Ron Wood turns 46. While most pop stars their age have entered semi-retirement (especially in the current pop climate, which seems to require that a major star should release a new record only every few years), the members of the Stones signed a new recording contract in 1991, and all four recorded solo albums over the next year. When asked what was up for the Stones during a promotional TV appearance in mid-1992, Watts replied in a somewhat bored voice that he supposed there would be another album and another tour.

And so there will be. Most performers may try the patience of most listeners in two years or less, but the Rolling Stones have not and probably will not any time in the near future. Perhaps the most amazing thing about the saga of the Rolling Stones is that, 30 years on, it isn't over yet.

# *Satisfaction, 1963-69*

The attraction felt by what sometimes seems to have been an entire generation of British young people to American pop music, especially R&B, after World War II is so well documented and has had such a lasting impact on the direction of Western music since the 1960s that it seems obvious and inevitable. But what was it that caused what was probably a tiny minority made up especially of working class youth in the UK to conceive an interest in a music completely alien to their culture and not immediately available on their radios or in their record shops?

It's hard to think of two cultures as different from each other as the one that produced Muddy Waters on a plantation in the southern United States in 1915 and the one that produced Mick Jagger, Keith Richards, and Brian Jones in a straitened, ration-stamp England in the early 1940s. Yet, today, it's easy to think of

Jagger, Richards, and Jones as Waters's musical off-spring, and they would be proud to be so considered.

Certainly, Britain was a country in upheaval in the post-war years, a nation — an empire — of long traditions shaken by bombings and deprivation, culturally altered by the very real invasion of friendly allies from the US. In the post-war years, the country's popular music was dominated by American songs and American performers. The very strangeness of American rural blues, urban R&B, and even be-bop jazz (Charlie Watts became a lifelong jazz fan) added to its appeal, making it part of a long European fascination for the exotic.

That may help explain why the future members of the Rolling Stones were attracted to American music, but it doesn't explain why they wanted to play it themselves, or why Brian Jones even went so far as to call himself Elmo Lewis, in honor of Elmore James.

One finds few clues to such idolatry by examining the musicians' early years, but one does find at least three essentially different types of people among the five men who achieved fame as the Rolling Stones.

Bill Wyman (born William Perks on October 24, 1936, in Lewisham, London) and Charlie Watts (born June 2, 1941, in Islington, London) were both working class children-made-good. Perks (who adopted Wyman as his stage name upon joining the Stones) came from a truly impoverished background, while Watts's father worked for British Rail. Both were hard-working, relatively ordinary young men for whom music was a hobby, but who understood the necessity for working hard to maintain what place in society they had.

*Top left:* The Rolling Stones in 1965, when they became international stars. Left to right: Bill Wyman, Keith Richards, Mick Jagger, Brian Jones, Charlie Watts.

*Above:* Charlie Watts was a graphic designer when he joined the Stones as their drummer more than 30 years ago.

*Right:* Bill Wyman, employing his trademark vertical bass-playing style, meets the crowd during an outdoor television appearance in the 1960s.

Wyman, by the time he auditioned to join a band called the Rollin' Stones on December 7, 1962, was 26 years old, married, and the father of an eight-month-old son. He was a store clerk by day who, by night, played the bass guitar in semi-professional groups for a few pounds. When Charlie Watts first played drums as a permanent member of the Rolling Stones on January 14, 1963 (it was around this time the 'g' was added), he had a promising job at a graphic design firm that seemed far more likely to contribute to his pension than this next in a succession of pub bands in which he'd played for fun.

But if Wyman and Watts represented the hard-working part of the working class, Brian Jones (born February 28, 1942, in Cheltenham, Gloucestershire) and Keith Richards (born December 18, 1943, in Dartford, Kent) were part of the more loutish, irresponsible element of that class. Jones was a near-classic case of the aimless teenage delinquent. Arguably more middle

class than working class, he showed devotion to music, but little else, except sex. When he fathered an illegitimate child at the age of 17, it was the first of at least five. Jones's attempts at responsibility and work were never even half-hearted, and it's hard to imagine what productive use he could have made of his life if he hadn't lucked into playing with a successful rock group. Even at that, he only lived to be 27.

Keith Richards wasn't the roue that Brian Jones was, but he showed little interest in anything other than the guitar after the start of his teens. Like Watts, he did study graphic design at art college. 'But basically I played guitar,' he later admitted.

Mick Jagger (born July 26, 1943, in Dartford, Kent) was the only one of the Stones to have real social and economic ambitions. When the band went professional, Wyman and Watts quit their jobs, and Jones and Richards were relatively unaffected. Jagger had to drop out of the London School of Economics.

*Far left:* Brian Jones fingers a chord on his trademark white Vox guitar.

*Above:* Keith Richards, looking almost unrecognizable as the Stones' guitarist in the 1960s.

*Right:* Brian Jones and Mick Jagger, rivals for leadership of the Stones, in 1966.

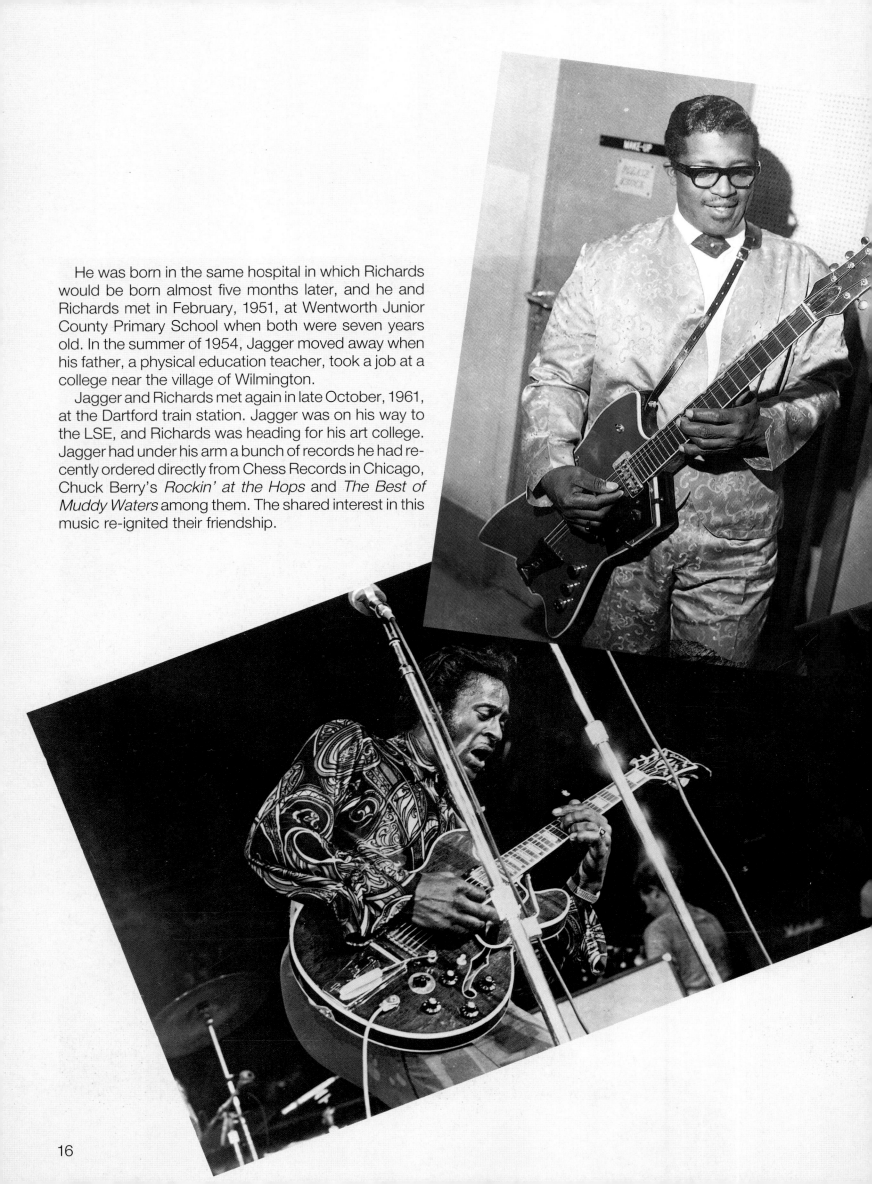

He was born in the same hospital in which Richards would be born almost five months later, and he and Richards met in February, 1951, at Wentworth Junior County Primary School when both were seven years old. In the summer of 1954, Jagger moved away when his father, a physical education teacher, took a job at a college near the village of Wilmington.

Jagger and Richards met again in late October, 1961, at the Dartford train station. Jagger was on his way to the LSE, and Richards was heading for his art college. Jagger had under his arm a bunch of records he had recently ordered directly from Chess Records in Chicago, Chuck Berry's *Rockin' at the Hops* and *The Best of Muddy Waters* among them. The shared interest in this music re-ignited their friendship.

*Left:* Bo Diddley, whose distinct sound influenced the Stones, for once not playing his square guitar.

*Below left:* Chuck Berry, whose 'Come On' was the Stones' first single.

*Above:* Muddy Waters, whose 'I Just Want to Make Love to You' appeared on the Stones' first album.

*Left:* Buddy Holly, whose 'Not Fade Away' was the Stones' first big hit.

Jagger and Richards didn't just get together and listen to records. Holed up in Jagger's house with Richards's friend Dick Taylor, they began trying to play and sing like their blues heroes. Eventually, the rehearsals continued with more friends – Bob Beckwith and Allen Etherington.

Brian Jones, meanwhile, had become obsessed with much the same music in Cheltenham and was determined to start a group. The only group then playing even an approximation of what Jones had in mind was a unit formed by Alexis Korner and called Blues Incorporated (whose drummer was a graphic designer named Charlie Watts) that began playing at the Ealing Jazz Club in the late winter of 1962. Jones first hitch-hiked into town to see the band on March 17, 1962, and by the following week was sitting in with them.

Jagger, Richards, and friends had also heard about the club and the band, and they turned up there on April 7, when they met Jones for the first time.

Placing an ad in *Jazz News* in search of players, Jones met pianist Ian Stewart in May. He began rehearsals with a variety of musicians at a local pub.

Meanwhile, Jagger and Richards had begun to get up onstage with Blues Incorporated regularly. But by June, they had quit the group and teamed up with Jones. This unnamed group then featured Jagger, Richards, Jones, Dick Taylor, Ian Stewart, and guitarist Geoff Bradford, but no drummer. Jones tried to persuade Charlie Watts to quit Blues Incorporated, but he wasn't interested. Instead, Jones found Tony Chapman through another advertisement. For a July 12 appearance at the Marquee Club, subbing for Blues Incorporated, Jones named the group 'The Rollin' Stones' after the Muddy Waters song 'Rollin' Stone Blues.' The still shifting lineup for the gig was Jagger, Richards, Jones, Taylor, Stewart, and drummer Mick Avory (later of the Kinks).

It earned them £20 and more bookings at the Marquee and at the Ealing Jazz Club through the summer and into the fall. By September, Dick Taylor, who had become the bass player, decided to return to school, and the Stones again advertised for a new member. Drummer Chapman brought Bill Wyman in, though it may have been more his superior equipment, including an amplifier that could also be used with one of the guitars, than his playing that initially guaranteed Wyman the job.

The drummer's chair continued to rotate until January, when Watts, who had quit Blues Incorporated, finally agreed to join the band. The first performance by the six-member Rolling Stones (Jagger, Richards, Jones, Stewart, Wyman, and Watts) took place on January 14, 1963, at the Flamingo in Soho. By February 24, they had secured an important residency at the Crawdaddy Club in Richmond.

With a permanent lineup and a steady place to play, the band next aspired to finding a manager and obtaining a record contract. They had circulated a demo tape in the fall of 1962, but found no takers. In January, February, and April, 1963, they made further recordings, but none of these have appeared officially on record.

*Above:* Mick Jagger playing the maracas at the Richmond Jazz Festival, August 11, 1963, one of the Stones' first major concerts.

*Right:* A more typical Stones venue for the period. Note the helmeted security guard in the lower left corner of the photo. Riot control was necessary at Stones concerts even early on.

Meanwhile, they began to attract attention in Richmond, earning a press write-up in the April 13 *Richmond and Twickenham Times*. On April 14, their gig was visited by all four of the Beatles, who were at this point the hottest group in the country. Most significantly, on April 28, 19-year-old Andrew Loog Oldham, a former Beatles publicist who had just begun renting an office from veteran manager Eric Easton, came down to see them. On May 1, the Rolling Stones signed a management contract with Easton and Oldham. That night, Oldham suggested to the band that Stewart, whose short hair and neat appearance contrasted with the rest of the group, didn't fit in and should be demoted from band member to road manager. They agreed. (Stewart would stay with the Stones, playing

piano on many of the recordings and later tours, until his death in 1985.)

Oldham also moved fast on the recording front, arranging for Dick Rowe of Decca Records (who turned down the Beatles in 1962) to see the Stones on May 6, which earned them a Decca recording contract. (Oldham also bought the Stones matching stage outfits in the manner of the Beatles; they didn't wear them.)

The Stones cut their first single, a version of Chuck Berry's 'Come On,' on May 10, 1963, at Olympic Studios in London. Oldham was the producer. Released on June 7, it got to a respectable Number 21 in the UK charts. By August, Bill Wyman decided things were going well enough that he could quit his day job.

By this time, the Stones' range of gigs was ex-

*Left:* The young Stones hardly look as outrageous and threatening as the image being created for them at the time.

*Right:* The Stones look more casual in this shot of a TV show performance in 1965.

*Below right:* Keith Richards experiments with the drum kit, though Brian Jones was the group's real multi-instrumentalist.

panding, they were being written up in the press, they were gaining TV and radio appearances, and they even had a fan club with 300 members.

On September 29, the Stones began their first national British 'package' tour as an opening act for the Everly Brothers and Bo Diddley. (Diddley was, of course, one of the Stones' heroes.) The tour ran through November 3. By then, the Stones' second single, 'I Wanna Be Your Man,' written for them by John Lennon and Paul McCartney, had been released. It did even better than their first, reaching Number 12.

Witnessing the success the Beatles were having writing original material, and realizing that the Stones would eventually run into trouble finding new R&B songs to cover, Oldham strongly encouraged Mick Jagger and Keith Richards to start writing songs, even taking the notorious action of locking them in a room until they had composed one. The composition of original music was a crucial element in the band's future. When one looks back now at the performers who emerged in the 1960s, it is those who generated their own material that succeeded in the long run. The Animals, for example, had many of the same qualities and influences as the Stones, but were completely dependent on outside songwriting. The same is true of the Dave Clark Five and numerous other, less popular Mersey Beat/British Invasion groups. In the long run, it was only the ones who could write their own hits who survived.

The first Jagger/Richards composition to turn up on record was 'That Girl Belongs to Yesterday,' released as a single by Gene Pitney in December, 1963. It was a Number Seven hit in the UK, and soon Jagger and Richards would be writing most of the songs for their own group.

The Stones continued to play shows, mainly around London, through the end of the year, then embarked on a second British package tour on January 6, 1964, opening for the Ronettes, that ran through the 27th. On the 10th, they released their first EP, 'The Rolling Stones.' (Though never very popular in the US, EPs – seven-inch discs usually containing four songs – were a successful record medium in the UK at the time.) It went to Number One on the EP chart.

A third British package tour, featuring the Stones and lesser acts, opened on February 8 and ran through March 7. On February 21, the Stones' third UK single, a cover of Buddy Holly's 'Not Fade Away,' was released. It became their first Top Ten hit, reaching Number Three. On March 6, it was released in the US on Decca's London Records label. The US was already reeling from the Beatles onslaught that had begun at the start of the year; now everyone with a British accent was racing up the charts. 'Not Fade Away' got to Number 48.

In the UK, the Stones released their first album on April 17. *The Rolling Stones* contained 12 tracks, one of which, 'Tell Me,' had been written by Jagger and Richards. Two others were credited to a group pseudonym, Nanker Phelge. (In mid-1965, the Stones discontinued use of the name and nearly every song they recorded thereafter was credited to Jagger/ Richards.) The album went to Number One and stayed there for 12 weeks – the only 12 weeks during 1964 that the Beatles were not on top of the LP chart.

*Left:* Mick Jagger dances at the Wimbledon Palais, August 14, 1964.

*Below:* The Beatles, shown performing on 'The Ed Sullivan Show' in February, 1964, conquered the US more than a year before the Stones finally broke through to stardom.

*Right:* Mick Jagger and fans at London Airport on June 1, 1964, as the Stones prepared to leave for their first US tour.

*Below right:* The Stones arrive in New York, June 1, 1964.

Indeed, the Stones had become the major alternative to the Beatles in Britain, capitalizing on a scruffy, rebellious image that contrasted with the Fab Four's milder persona. Similarly, their harder-edged, more blues-based music served fans who wanted something rougher than the music of the Beatles, which included ballads and material that was more pop. And the Stones had earned their own crowd of screaming fans, with their shows turning increasingly disruptive.

In the US the Stones had not yet emerged from the pack of Beatle followers, however. A version of their album was released on the London label in May with the title, *England's Newest Hitmakers*. US and UK record company practices differed at this time in that, in the UK it was considered something of a consumer rip-off to put on an album a track that also had been released as a single. In the US including the single on the LP was considered simple marketing common sense. Accordingly, London substituted 'Not Fade Away' for 'Mona' on their version of the LP. It went to Number 11.

With an album to promote, the Stones went on tour in North America between June 2 and 20. Though they

were well received in New York and California,
Nebraska and Pennsylvania didn't know what to make
of them – that is, when residents of those states
showed up to see them at all. A second US (but not UK)
single, 'Tell Me,' released during the tour, became the
Stones' first US Top 40 hit, reaching Number 24. Significantly, it was also the first time a Jagger/Richards
composition was a hit for the Stones.

On June 26, the Stones released their fourth UK
single, a cover of the Womack Brothers' 'It's All Over
Now.' Not surprisingly, it became the Stones' first
Number One hit single, and the first of four UK Number
Ones for them in a row. Released in the US in July, it got
to Number 26. But a fourth US single, 'Time Is On My
Side,' finally broke through to the US Top Ten, reaching
Number Six after being released on September 26.

The Stones returned to the US in late October after
another UK tour and their first European tour to find
things much improved over their first American outing.
A second US album, *12 X 5*, cobbled together from the
band's recent singles and their second UK EP, reached
Number Three. A new US-only single, 'Heart of Stone,'
reached Number 19.

By the end of 1964, the Rolling Stones were firmly en-
sconced as the second biggest rock band in Britain,
and they had found widespread success in the US and
elsewhere. Nineteen sixty-five, however, was their
breakthrough year, not only because they were able to
match their UK success in America, but because they
did it with their original compositions – songs that
expressed their dangerous image.

The Stones began 1965 with shows in Ireland and

London, plus some TV appearances. On January 16, they released their second UK album, *The Rolling Stones No. 2*. Again, it was dominated by cover material, though three of the 12 songs were Stones' originals. The album was another Number One hit. In the US, London Records altered the album, substituting five tracks for its version, *The Rolling Stones, Now!*, which was released in February. This album hit Number Five.

The Stones embarked on a Far East tour in January and February, and stopped off at RCA Studios in Hollywood, which had become one of their favorite places to record, both on their way out and on their way back. These sessions resulted in a new UK and US single, the original composition 'The Last Time,' which Richards would later describe as the first song he and Jagger hadn't been embarrassed to present to the band. The single was an automatic Number One hit in the UK, and got to Number Nine in the US.

The Stones embarked on a two-week British tour on

*Left:* The Stones arrive by bus at one of their many concert venues in the mid-1960s.

*Above:* The Stones on 'The Ed Sullivan Show,' taped September 9, 1966 and broadcast September 11. They played 'Paint It Black,' 'Lady Jane,' and 'Have You Seen Your Mother, Baby, Standing in the Shadow?'

March 5, then went to Europe for three weeks starting March 26. Their third North American tour commenced April 23 in Quebec and took them around Canada and the States through May 30. They were most of the way through the tour when they stopped off at RCA Studios for more recording sessions.

The Stones could do no wrong in Britain, but it took '(I Can't Get No) Satisfaction,' recorded May 12-13, 1965, and released in the US on June 5, to establish them firmly in America. It was the first, but not the last time that the Stones would move to a new plateau by managing to write and record a great rock 'n' roll song. Not only did 'Satisfaction' top the charts for four weeks, but the album in which it was included (in the US that is, not in the UK), *Out of Our Heads*, also went to Number One in the US. (The UK version of *Out of Our Heads*, which shared only six tracks with the US version, reached Number Two.)

For the next two years, the Stones consistently reached the upper echelons of the charts and played to sell-out crowds everywhere, all the while turning out a stunning series of rock classics. Their follow-up to 'Satisfaction' was 'Get Off of My Cloud,' which also topped the American and British charts. The US-only album *December's Children* reached Number Four and contained the ballad single 'As Tears Go By,' which hit Number Six. (In the UK, the song, as recorded by Jagger's girlfriend Marianne Faithfull, had been a Number Nine hit a year and a half before, and thus was not released as a Stones single.)

Nineteen sixty-six brought the driving '19th Nervous Breakdown,' which hit Number Two on both sides of the Atlantic. In March, London Records released the first Stones compilation, *Big Hits (High Tide and Green Grass)*, which reached Number Three and, at 99 weeks, had a longer chart life than any Rolling Stones album in the band's history except a similar, more extensive compilation called *Hot Rocks*, released in 1972.

Then came the all-original *Aftermath* album (the 14-track UK version shared 10 songs with the 11-track US version), another British Number One that spent two weeks at Number Two in the US. Then the gloomy single 'Paint It Black' topped the UK and US charts. 'Mother's Little Helper,' released as a single only in the

US, got to Number Eight, perhaps restrained by its drug-related subject matter. The Stones' final single of 1966 was 'Have You Seen Your Mother, Baby, Standing in the Shadow?,' which became their ninth straight Top Ten hit in the UK, their eighth straight in the US. And the group rounded off the year by issuing a version of *Big Hits* in the UK and a concert album, *Got Live If You Want It*, in the US.

But one reason for the two-year rule in pop music is a kind of mutual audience and performer exhaustion. Call it overexposure or life in the fast lane or burn-out, but two years seems to be all most people can take of the pressure of stardom at the top.

The group had completed its fifth North American tour in July, 1966, followed by a British tour that concluded in October, 1966. The album *Between the Buttons*, released in January, 1967, marked a retreat from their hard rock sound to a more eclectic pop approach in keeping with changing trends. But when the Stones ran into censorship trouble with their first single of the year, 'Let's Spend the Night Together' (and as a result

flipped it over for the US Number One 'Ruby Tuesday'), strain was starting to show.

On February 5, the British tabloid newspaper *News of the World* published a story claiming that Mick Jagger had taken LSD. The story was in fact mistakenly based on a conversation a reporter had had with Brian Jones in May, 1966. An enraged Jagger sued the paper on February 7. On February 12, acting on a tip from *News of the World*, police raided Keith Richards's home looking for drugs, and arrested both the guitarist and Jagger.

It was the beginning of a hard year for the Stones. Jagger and Richards were brought up on drug charges – Jagger for possession of amphetamine pills obtained legally in Italy, Richards for allowing drugs to be taken in his home. Found guilty in June, they were let off on appeal in July. The ordeal was worsened by Brian Jones's arrest for drugs in May.

The Stones managed a European tour from March 25 to April 17, but their accumulated problems would make it their last for two and a half years. They also

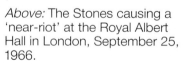

*Above:* The Stones causing a 'near-riot' at the Royal Albert Hall in London, September 25, 1966.

*Above right:* Mick Jagger looks unconcerned in this photo by Cecil Beaton taken in July, 1967, even though he is out on bail after his drug conviction, pending appeal.

*Right:* Mick Jagger and Keith Richards on May 10, 1967, the day they were indicted on drug charges.

recorded sporadically, though the combination of legal distractions and the changes in popular taste led them in doubtful directions. When their next album, *Their Satanic Majesties Request* (their first since a break with Andrew Loog Oldham) was released in December, it was greeted as a rip-off of *Sgt. Pepper's Lonely Hearts Club Band*, and sales fell off quickly.

Brian Jones, found guilty of possession of marijuana, eventually got off with three years' probation and a fine, but his fragile health and temperament were affected by the ordeal, and things only got worse when he was arrested a second time in May, 1968.

The same week, however, the Stones' comeback commenced with the release of 'Jumpin' Jack Flash,' a powerful return to their hard rock style. The follow-up album, *Beggars Banquet*, originally set for release in July, was held up due to a dispute over the album cover, which the Stones wanted to depict a bathroom wall with the song titles as graffiti. They lost the fight (though the original cover would be restored when the album came out on CD), but the LP didn't appear until December.

*Below:* A shot from the early 1969 David Bailey photo session that was among the last with Brian Jones.

*Right:* The new Stones lineup introduced at a photo session/press conference held in Hyde Park, London, June 13, 1969. New guitarist Mick Taylor is second from left.

The Stones were determined to return to concert work in 1969, but Brian Jones's health and legal problems continued to imperil such plans. On June 8, the conflict was resolved when Jones left the band, citing musical differences. The Stones then hired 21-year-old guitarist Mick Taylor, a member of John Mayall's Bluesbreakers, as a replacement, and announced plans for a free concert in Hyde Park, London, on July 5.

Brian Jones drowned in his swimming pool just after midnight on July 3. On the 4th, the Stones released their first post-Jones single, 'Honky Tonk Women,' a worldwide Number One hit. On July 5, they went ahead with the Hyde Park concert, dedicating it to Jones.

*Top left:* Marianne Faithfull and Mick Jagger appear at Marlborough Street Magistrates' Court on May 29, 1969, the day after they were arrested for possession of marijuana.

*Left:* Anita Pallenberg, Keith Richards, and their eight-day-old son Marlon leave King's College Hospital, Dulwich, London, August 18, 1969.

*Above:* Keith Richards and Mick Jagger onstage at Madison Square Garden in New York during the Stones' first American tour in three years, November 28, 1969.

The Rolling Stones' sixth North American tour, which opened on November 7, more than three years since their last one, presented them at both their best and worst. With the Beatles out of the way as a concert act, the Stones were hailed as the biggest live rock act ever – as their tour announcer put it, 'the greatest rock 'n' roll band in the world.' Their new album, *Let It Bleed*, was a substantial hit.

But the 1969 tour will also be remembered for its final, disastrous show, the massive free concert in Altamont, California, at which the Hells Angels motorcycle gang, hired as security, brutalized the crowd and killed a young man in front of the stage while the Stones played. If the Stones didn't bear as much direct responsibility for this horror as some claimed, their public image, nevertheless, expressed both in their music and in their lifestyles, seemed consistent with it. And though they went on to further triumphs, no one would ever let them forget that show.

# It's Only Rock 'N' Roll, 1970-79

If 1969 was the most traumatic year in the Rolling Stones' history, it's no surprise that they opened the 1970s quietly. For one thing, they needed to make business changes. Their management had been left in the hands of New York accountant Allen Klein after the departure of Andrew Loog Oldham, and in July, 1970, they started legal proceedings against him. The eventual settlement would leave Klein in possession of all Rolling Stones recordings made between 1963 and 1970. At the same time, the Stones' contract with Decca expired with the release of a live album, *Get Yer Ya-Ya's Out!*, taken from the 1969 tour. The Stones decided to launch their own label, with distribution through Atlantic Records.

Other than the live album, the year passed without any new Stones recordings being released, though the Stones did do some recording in the early summer. They also embarked on their first European tour since 1967 on August 31, 1970, in Sweden. The tour ran through October 11. The Stones followed it with their first full-fledged British tour since 1966 in March, 1971.

The UK tour was a 'farewell' tour in the sense that the Stones had decided to move to France to avoid the high British taxes. Many other rockers would become tax exiles in the 1970s, but the Stones led the way, moving south in April, 1971. The same month, they released their first single on Rolling Stones Records, 'Brown Sugar,' followed by the album *Sticky Fingers*.

*Left:* The Rolling Stones at the 4000-seat Roundhouse in London, March 14, 1971, the final date of the farewell tour of Britain before they moved to France.

*Above:* Mick Jagger at the Roundhouse gig.

*Right:* Bill Wyman. Over the years his clothes and hair styles changed, but the poker face and static stage posture never did.

Although the Stones had been one of the most popular bands of the 1960s, it was only in the 1970s, when they didn't have the Beatles to compete with any more, and when they possessed a priceless legacy as rock progenitors, that they really came into their own as successful musicians. *Sticky Fingers* was their best-selling album up to this point: It went to Number One for four weeks in the US and stayed in the charts for 62 weeks.

If the group was achieving unprecedented success, it was also, through Mick Jagger, making inroads into

*Top left:* Andy Warhol's cover design for the 1971 *Sticky Fingers* album. The zipper worked on the original copies.

*Left:* The Rolling Stones (left to right: Keith Richards, Charlie Watts, Bill Wyman, Mick Jagger, and Mick Taylor), at a photo session for their *Sticky Fingers* album, released in April, 1971.

*Above:* Nicaraguan beauty Bianca Perez Morena de Macias became Mrs. Mick Jagger in St. Tropez on May 12, 1971. They were divorced in 1979.

society. On May 12, 1971, Jagger gave up his bachelor status when he married Bianca Perez Morena de Macias in St. Tropez. The bride was a 21-year-old 'society girl' (as the *Daily Mirror* put it) from Nicaragua, and Jagger even took instruction in the Catholic religion in preparation for the marriage.

After the honeymoon, recording sessions commenced on July 10 in a mobile recording studio set up in Keith Richards's home in Villefranche sur Mer. They continued through September. More than 20 tracks were recorded, and the Stones planned to release a double album called *Tropical Disease* in February, 1972. But in February, the Stones were still in a Los Angeles studio doing overdubs and mixing, and the album didn't appear until May 26, by which time it had acquired the title *Exile on Main Street*.

*Below:* Mick Jagger emotes during the Stones' 1972 American tour.

*Below right:* The Stones at Wembley Empire Pool in London, September 7, 1973, during their European tour, with a three-piece horn section.

*Sticky Fingers* may have been the Stones' best seller up to the release of *Tattoo You* in 1978, but *Exile* was their best-reviewed album ever. The album has a somewhat murky mix, but that was part of what critics loved about it, and even 20 years later, it frequently turns up on lists of the best rock 'n' roll records of all time.

The Stones embarked on their seventh North American tour on June 3 to promote it. By this time, the

nationwide tour circuit in the US, which had been in its infancy when the Stones first appeared in 1964, had become well-organized. Even the 1969 tour had consisted of only 22 shows in 17 different locations in just under a month. The 1972 tour ran nearly two months and included 48 shows, most in indoor sports arenas holding 10,000 to 20,000 people, though large outdoor venues such as Robert F. Kennedy Memorial Stadium in Washington, DC, were also included.

On November 25, 1972, the Stones convened in Kingston, Jamaica, to record a new album at Dynamic Studios. Sessions went on until December 21. The Stones began touring again on January 18, 1973, when they played a benefit concert for relief of Nicaragua, which had recently suffered an earthquake, at the Forum in Los Angeles. This mini-US tour was continued with a few dates in Hawaii on the way to the Stones' first tour of the Far East since 1966.

In June, 1973, Keith Richards was again arrested on drug charges in England at the house he maintained in London. Eventually, Richards would plead guilty to possession of marijuana, Chinese heroin, and Mandrax tablets, and be fined.

If Richards got off easily this time, his increasing addiction to heroin seems to have begun affecting the band's performance. The new album, *Goat's Head Soup*, released on August 31, though it sold predictably well, seemed to have less of Richards's input, and the songs suffered. In later years, it would be admitted that

the 'Jagger/Richards' composing credit might more accurately have read 'Jagger' for much of the middle part of the 1970s.

Nevertheless, Richards was able to function onstage despite his addiction, and the Stones continued to engage in periodic tours of various parts of the world in turn. On September 1, they launched a tour of Europe that ran through October 19.

On November 13, the Stones went to Musicland Studios in Munich to begin work on a new album. But they were not accompanied by Mick Taylor, who was said to be suffering from a 'mysterious illness.' They worked for 11 days, then broke for the holidays without finishing, returning on January 14, 1974, for an additional two weeks. The first result of these efforts was a single, 'It's Only Rock 'N' Roll (But I Like It),' released July 26. Lacking a tour or an album to cross-promote it, and despite a music video that showed the group cavorting in sailor suits amidst a sea of bubbles, the single only got to Number 16 in the US.

*Top left:* The Stones, in sailor suits, at the shoot for the video of 'It's Only Rock 'N' Roll' in New York, early summer, 1974.

*Above:* The video was shot inside an inflated room that was filled with foam – so much that the Stones (except Watts, who was on the drum riser) nearly drowned.

*Right:* Jagger's live vocals recorded at the video shoot differ from the released version of 'It's Only Rock 'N' Roll.'

It was also considered a rather uninspired effort, an opinion also expressed about the *It's Only Rock 'N' Roll* album when it appeared three months later. Though it did manage to hit Number One, the LP lasted in the US charts only 20 weeks – a shorter period of time than any Stones album ever.

In November, the Rolling Stones held a three-day band meeting in Switzerland to discuss future plans, and they seem to have agreed to do a new album that would be ready for release in time for a summer tour of the US. As it turned out, things did not go according to plan.

The Stones did return to Musicland Studios on December 7 to begin recording the new album, but they suffered an unhappy surprise when Mick Taylor announced on December 12 that he was leaving the group. Reportedly, Taylor was unhappy that he was not receiving songwriting credit on Stones songs, although he denied such accounts and simply said that he wanted to accept an offer from former Cream bassist Jack Bruce to join his band.

The Stones managed to lay down tracks for a couple of songs during their one week in the studio, but the Taylor announcement made things difficult. Mick Jagger tried to put a light face on the matter by telling the press, 'No doubt we can find a brilliant 6' 3" blond guitarist who can do his own makeup.' But it wouldn't be that easy.

On January 22, 1975, the Stones set up shop in their own mobile recording facilities in Rotterdam, The Netherlands, though nothing they recorded turned up on the next album. They then returned to Musicland on March 22 and spent a couple of weeks recording there. These sessions doubled as guitar auditions, with the players including Jeff Beck, Harvey Mandel, Ron Wood, and Wayne Perkins. Though the material eventually would turn up on record, the band seems to have decided not to release an album at this time.

What that meant, with American tour plans much advanced, was that the Stones would have to hit the road without a second guitarist and without an album to promote. On March 27, Chris Spedding confirmed that he had been asked to join the band, but had had to decline due to other commitments. On April 14, it was announced that Ron Wood, guitarist for the Faces (with Rod Stewart), would join the Stones for the 1975 tour only.

*Below:* Ron Wood (left) joins
the Stones during one of their
six shows at Madison Square
Garden, June, 1975.

*Below:* Ron Wood (left) joins the Stones during one of their six shows at Madison Square Garden, June, 1975.

Scenes from the Madison Square Garden shows in 1975:

*Left:* The Stones' staging got more elaborate in the 1970s. Here, Jagger exhibits his fondness for inflatable objects.

*Below left:* Unlike Mick Taylor, Ron Wood got a microphone. Here he approaches it, as Mick Jagger and Keith Richards belt it out on theirs.

*Right:* A good view of the state-of-the-art stage lighting, circa 1975.

*Below:* Eric Clapton (second from left) joins the Stones on June 22, as they perform 'Sympathy For the Devil' as an encore.

On May 1, in what is still remembered as the best publicity stunt of the Rolling Stones' career, the band turned up in New York City playing on a flatbed truck to announce the dates for the Tour of the Americas. The tour was set to start June 1 in Baton Rouge, Louisiana, and conclude on August 21 in Caracas, Venezuela, with a total of 58 dates, 16 of which would take place in South America. (The South American dates were later cancelled and more US dates were added.)

Meanwhile, the absence of a new Stones record was made up for by Allen Klein, who released *Metamorphosis* on June 6. Though both Decca and London had issued various repackagings of Stones material since 1970, this was the first album to consist of previously unreleased tracks. Rolling Stones Records countered a week later with *Made in the Shade*, a greatest hits record made up of tracks from 1971-1974.

The 1975 tour was the Stones' biggest yet. It featured a stage in a flower petal shape designed by Robin Wagner. Many of the dates were in stadiums, and the Stones did six shows at Madison Square Garden in New York, and five at the Forum in Los Angeles. The real end date turned out to be Rich Stadium in Buffalo on August 8. The tour was marred only by the arrest of Keith Richards, who was stopped by police while driving in Fordyce, Arkansas, and charged with possession of an offensive weapon that Richards described as a penknife.

In the fall, the Stones returned to work on the new album at Mountain Recording Studios in Montreux, France, and at Musicland, and they planned a European tour. Though still a member of the Faces, Ron Wood participated in the recording sessions, which concluded on December 16.

On December 18, Rod Stewart, lead singer of the Faces, whose solo career always overshadowed the group, finally quit, effectively leading to the Faces' demise. On January 10, 1976, the Stones held what was described as 'a formal business meeting' with Ron Wood in New York, and on February 28, three weeks after Wood had participated in the photo session for the next album cover, it was announced that he had become a permanent member of the Rolling Stones.

The Stones' 1976 European tour was announced on March 12. It would begin on April 28 and run through June 23. On April 20, the long-promised new album, *Black and Blue*, was released. Its chart showing was better than that of *It's Only Rock 'N' Roll*, staying at Number One in the US for four weeks, but its 24-week chart run was still short for a Stones album.

The tour was particularly eventful for Keith Richards, who was arrested again in England on May 19 after an auto accident when LSD and cocaine were found in his car. Eventually, he was fined £750. In early June, Richards's 10-week-old daughter Tara by his common law wife Anita Pallenberg died of a flu virus. Nevertheless, Richards was able to finish out the tour.

On August 21, the Stones played one last date, a show at the Knebworth Festival in England before 200,000 people. In the fall, Mick Jagger and Ron Wood began sifting through tapes of the tour to assemble the Stones' first live album in seven years.

Since 1967, Keith Richards had frequently fallen afoul of the law in connection with his drug-taking, but had always gotten off without serious consequences. He had also been able to maintain his presence in the Rolling Stones as his addiction to heroin increased in the 1970s, even if Mick Jagger was forced to shoulder the bulk of songwriting and organizing work.

But Richards's luck ran out on February 27, 1977, in Toronto, where the Stones had gone in order to record a side's worth of live tracks in a local club for their upcoming concert album. A police raid of Richards's hotel room turned up enough heroin to come under the definition of possession for re-sale, so that Richards could be prosecuted not just as a user but as a dealer as well.

The Stones nevertheless played at the El Mocambo club, capacity 300, on March 4 and 5. Richards's hearing came on March 7, when he faced possible life imprisonment on the charges. Richards was forced to stay in Toronto until April 1, when he was remanded on bail until a scheduled court appearance in June. He then flew to New York, where he began to undergo treatment for heroin addiction. His hearing was postponed several times, and was finally set for December 2.

The Rolling Stones' live album, *Love You Live*, was released on September 16. It was a reasonable success, its Number Five chart placing one notch above that managed by the Stones' two previous live albums, though it stayed in the charts only 17 weeks and only achieved a gold (500,000 copies) certification rather than platinum (1,000,000 copies).

*Left:* Keith Richards during the 1976 European tour, the last one he performed while a heroin addict.

*Below:* Fashion plate Mick Jagger returns to the maracas during the 1976 European tour.

*Some Girls* the first Rolling Stones album to spin off three hits.

The album probably was also aided by the controversy that surrounded it. First, there was the cover, a parody of lingerie ads that featured various famous faces. The Stones would be forced to alter it when legal challenges came up. Then there was the title track, on which Mick Jagger made a variety of remarks about a variety of types of girls, one of which was, 'Black girls just like to get f---ed all night.' Howls of protest went up, but Jagger was unperturbed. 'If you can't take a joke, it's too f---ing bad,' he said.

Indeed, it was hard to take the controversy seriously, and fans felt almost nostalgic about the Stones' ability to stir people up once again. The album became the Stones' biggest seller. It topped the US charts for two weeks, but stayed in the listings for 82 weeks. By 1984, it had sold four million copies.

The album's popularity was also aided by the Stones' third American tour of the 1970s, which commenced on June 10 in Lakeland, Florida, and ended on July 26 (Mick Jagger's 35th birthday) in Oakland, California, playing fewer dates than previous tours, but playing them for the most part in football stadiums.

In October, the Stones commenced recording sessions for a new album at Pathe-Marconi, EMI Studios, in Paris. The sessions continued until December 21, with a break at the start of December for Keith Richards's court date in Toronto. Richards's case was remanded to a higher court with a hearing in February, 1978, which was later delayed until March, when a trial date was set for October 23.

Despite this, the Stones managed to record a large number of tracks, working until March 3 in Paris. With the trial date set for the fall, they were able to schedule a US concert tour for the summer.

'Miss You,' the first single from the new album, was released May 19, followed by the album *Some Girls* on June 9. In 1967, when the Stones had suffered legal troubles, it seemed to affect their music and their popularity negatively; in 1978, the opposite was the case. 'Miss You' was essentially a disco track, and it was released when disco was at its height. It hit Number One, becoming the Stones' biggest single in five years, and it was followed by a second Top Ten hit, the ballad 'Beast of Burden,' and by a Top 40 hit, 'Shattered,' making

On October 23 in Toronto, Keith Richards pleaded guilty to possession of heroin, a charge plea-bargained down from the earlier charge of trafficking in heroin. Judge Lloyd Graburn, after hearing Richards's lawyer describe the guitarist's battles with heroin dating back to 1969, sentenced Richards to a one-year probation and ordered him to give a benefit concert at the National Institute for the Blind within six months.

The Stones began work on their next album in January, 1979, at Compass Point Studios in Nassau, The Bahamas. Though a great deal of material was recorded, only four of the tracks would be released.

On April 22, Keith Richards led a band called the New Barbarians, featuring Ron Wood, at two shows at the Civic Auditorium in Oshawa, Ontario, fulfilling his court sentence. Thus assembled, the band embarked on a US tour – the first non-Stones tour for a Stones member – starting on April 24 in Ann Arbor, Michigan, and continuing through May 21 at the Forum in Los Angeles. Mick Jagger, meanwhile, was busy getting divorced from his wife Bianca.

On June 18, the Stones got back together at Pathe-Marconi to continue work on their next album. They worked through October 19 (with interruptions for more divorce court dates by Jagger and an appearance at Knebworth by the New Barbarians).

It wasn't quite as dramatic an end to a decade as the 1960s had been for the Stones, but the end of the 1970s found them, despite problems, as successful as ever. They had toured the world several times, released a stream of top selling albums, and continued to fascinate their fans. Surprisingly for an act of their pre-

eminence, they had continued to work steadily, never breaking for long from the next tour or the next album, always maintaining the momentum of their career.

And though rock 'n' roll traditionally has been thought of as a young man's game, as the 1970s ended, the Stones, who ranged in age from 36 to 43, seemed ready to continue. An especially bright spot was Keith Richards's return from addiction, which seemed to eliminate the major cloud from the band's future, although his return to action would bring its own problems with it.

# *Mixed Emotions, 1980-Present*

In January, 1980, as the Rolling Stones completed 17 years in existence, they were remarkable not only in having survived so long, but also in having continued as a popular success throughout the 1970s. In that decade, they had placed 12 albums – their entire new output, plus live albums and compilations – in the US Top Ten, and all six of their new studio albums had gone to Number One. And though they were not as much of a singles act as they had been in the 1960s, they could still claim six Top Ten singles in the 1970s, three of which went to Number One. In addition to this, of course, there were sell-out tours on a regular basis all over the world.

As their third decade began, the Stones simply continued on in the consistent, if volatile manner they always had. On February 18, 1980, Bill Wyman told interviewer David Wigg of the *Daily Express* that he intended to quit the Rolling Stones in 1982, by which time he would have served as their bass player for 20 years. 'I know I don't want to be a middle-aged rock 'n' roller,' said the 43-year-old Wyman. 'Probably some people think I am already.'

On June 20, Rolling Stones Records released a new single, 'Emotional Rescue,' the title track from the new Stones album, which appeared three days later. Like 'Miss You,' 'Emotional Rescue' was set to a disco beat, and it even featured the unusual novelty of a vocal sung partially in falsetto by Mick Jagger. It hit Number Three in the charts. The *Emotional Rescue* album was also a substantial hit, spending seven weeks at Number One, longer than any previous Rolling Stones LP.

In September, Mick Jagger and Keith Richards began working on a new album in London, though, rather than recording all-new material, they sifted through outtakes from previous recording sessions. New recording, however, did commence at Pathe-Marconi Studios in October, and continued through November.

*Left:* A view of the giant outdoor stage set used on the Stones' 1981 American tour.

*Below:* Bill Wyman displays his usual level of excitement at the Meadowlands Arena in East Rutherford, New Jersey, November 6, 1981.

*Right:* Mick Jagger cribs a guitar chord from Keith Richards during the 1981 tour. Jagger began playing guitar occasionally onstage as of 1978.

*Below right:* Keith Richards, Mick Jagger, and Ron Wood onstage, 1981.

In March, 1981, Rolling Stones Records released *Sucking in the Seventies*, a new compilation album with a couple of unreleased tracks. The album broke the Stones' 13-year, 26-album string of Top Ten hits, peaking only at Number 15.

The album did, however, give the Stones breathing space to finish their new album and plan their next tour. Spring came and went without any announcement, but on August 26, Jagger appeared at an empty JFK Stadium in Philadelphia to alert the press to the Stones' 1981 US tour. The tour would begin on September 25, at JFK, and continue through December 19, making it the longest and largest concert series the Stones had ever undertaken.

The following week, the Stones released their new album, *Tattoo You*. Seven of its 11 tracks, including the single, 'Start Me Up,' had been recorded in 1979 during the *Emotional Rescue* sessions, while the remaining four came from the fall 1980 sessions.

But *Tattoo You* didn't sound like an album of outtakes. Beginning with 'Start Me Up,' a mid-tempo rock anthem to rank with the Stones' best, the album was hailed as a return to form even more than *Some Girls* had been. Abandoning the disco inflections of the previous two albums, and much more assured than the somewhat flabby mid-1970s efforts, *Tattoo You* was the best Stones album since the band's triumphs of 1971-72, *Sticky Fingers* and *Exile on Main Street*.

*Left:* A good view of the revolving indoor stage set for the 1981 tour.

*Below:* Mick Jagger's 1981 sporting-goods look. Ron Wood just looks like a rock star.

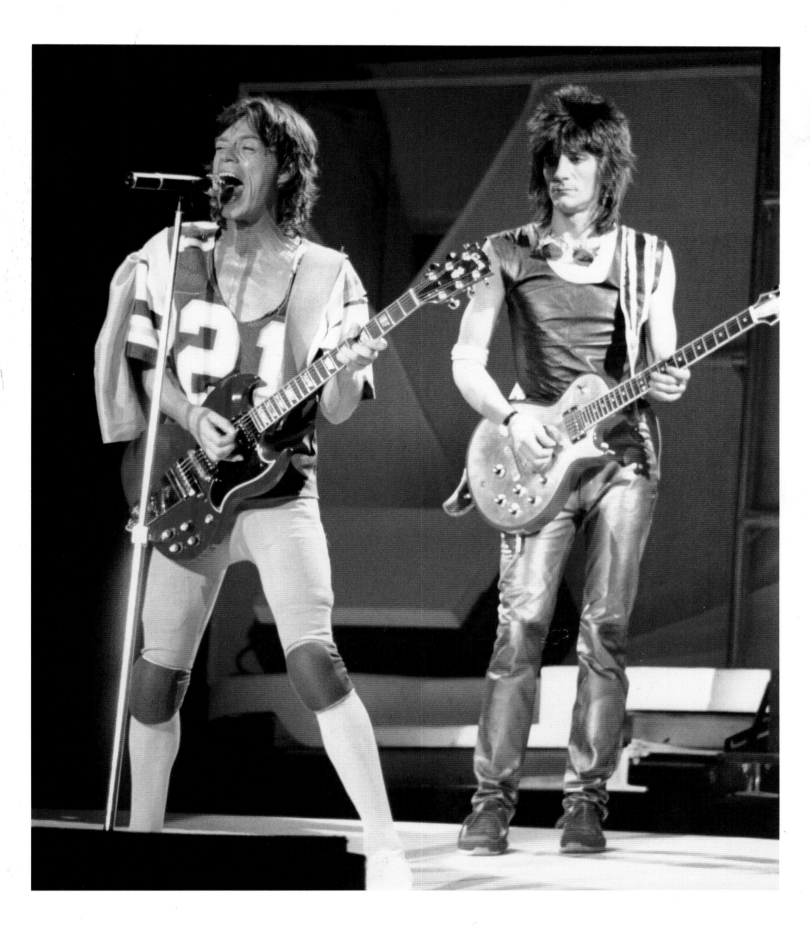

*Left:* Keith Richards strikes Rock Guitarist Pose Number 1 during the 1981 tour.

*Below:* Thirty-eight years old and still skinny, Mick Jagger tans himself onstage in 1981.

*Right:* Jagger in mid-strut across the 1981 stadium stage.

And with a massive tour to promote it, the album was an enormous success, its sales of three million copies in the US second only to *Some Girls* as the group's best seller. 'Start Me Up' reached Number Two and was followed by 'Waiting on a Friend' (Number 13) and 'Hang Fire' (Number 20).

The tour, which played before audiences sometimes exceeding 100,000 per show (146,000 at Candlestick Park in San Francisco), was played out on a stage (actually, there were three of them used in different cities) that was 50 feet high and 200 feet wide. In all, over two million people saw the Stones perform in America at 50 concerts, and the tour grossed over $50 million.

On April 28, Mick Jagger announced plans for a European tour to start in June in Rotterdam. It actually opened on May 26 in Aberdeen, Scotland, and ran through July 25.

*Below:* Keith Richards and Mick Jagger (with Bill Wyman in the background) onstage during the 1982 European tour, the Stones' last for seven years.

*Right:* A colorful Mick Jagger outdoors in Europe, 1982.

*Still Life*, the Rolling Stones' fourth live album, was released on June 1, with a single version of the old Smokey Robinson and the Miracles hit 'Going to a Go Go.' The album went to Number Five in the US and stayed in the charts for 23 weeks, a showing comparable to other Stones live albums. The single went to Number 25.

When the Rolling Stones played the final concert of their 1982 European tour on July 25, the day before Mick Jagger's 39th birthday, there didn't seem to be any reason to think that it was the last the world would see of the group onstage, even if Bill Wyman made good on this threat to retire. Rather, the band's very

longevity would have seemed to suggest that their pattern of recording and touring would continue indefinitely. Like a married couple that had been together almost 20 years, one would suppose that, if they hadn't broken up by now, they never would.

In fact, however, it would be seven years before the Stones would tour again, and in that time most people, the Stones included, would think the band had split up.

In the short term, things went on as they always had. In October and November, the Stones worked on a new album at Pathe-Marconi Studios. The album, titled *Undercover*, was finished up at Compass Point Studios the following May.

*Left:* The ultra-glamorous Jerry Hall and Mick Jagger have been an item since 1977.

*Below:* Jagger, seen here lolling in the bleachers of one of the stadiums the Stones played in the 1980s, took an unusually active role in organizing their tours and stage presentations.

*Below right:* Bill Wyman, standing between Eric Clapton and Jeff Beck, participated in the series of ARMS benefit shows to fight multiple sclerosis in the fall of 1983.

If it's possible to date the start of cracks in the Stones' structure, that date may be August, 1983, when the Stones signed a contract with Columbia Records reportedly for $28 million and four albums. (The contract would not take effect until the Stones finished off their Atlantic deal, for which they owed one more album.) It would later turn out that Columbia had signed Jagger as a solo artist as well and that they would encourage him to record separately. They did not sign any of the other Stones separately.

A new single, 'Undercover of the Night,' was released on November 1, followed by the album *Undercover* on November 7. The single reached Number Nine in the US and Number One in the UK, while the album hit Number Four in the US and Number Three in the UK. (A second single, 'She Was Hot,' reached Number 44 in the US and Number 42 in the UK). The album was certified platinum, but its relatively low chart placing (it was the first new studio album by the Stones to miss the Number One slot in the US since 1969) and its less-than-six-months residence in the charts indicated some slippage in the Stones' popularity.

The Stones supported the album with promotional videos sent to MTV and other outlets, but they did not tour. In the spring of 1984, Jagger began writing songs and doing demos for what would become his first solo album. Jagger spent the second week of May in New York's A&R Studio, recording the vocals to the new Jacksons single, 'State of Shock,' with Michael Jackson. When it was released the following month, the single reached Number Three in the US and Number 14 in the UK.

*Left:* Mick Jagger duets with Tina Turner on a medley of 'State of Shock' and 'It's Only Rock 'N' Roll' at the Live Aid benefit concert in Philadelphia, July 13, 1985.

*Above:* Ron Wood and Keith Richards support Bob Dylan at the close of the Live Aid concert.

On July 2, Rolling Stones Records released its final album under its contract with Atlantic, a compilation called *Rewind (1971-1984)* that gathered together various hits, some of which had already turned up on previous hits collections. Clearly a contractual obligation record, *Rewind* reached only Number 86 in the US, though it got to Number 23 in the UK, where a reissued 'Brown Sugar' hit Number 58 in the singles chart. In the US, 'Miss You' was reissued, but it didn't chart. (Later, a video version of *Rewind* would be released, featuring Wyman as a nightwatchman in a museum picking his way through dusty Stones lore, including Jagger himself, encased in glass.)

In September, Jagger went to work on his first solo album, delaying proposed work on the Stones' first Columbia album. Having completed the record, *She's the Boss,* Jagger spent five weeks in Brazil with Julien Temple in November and December, shooting a long-form video to promote the record.

Jagger and Temple conceived a screenplay about a rock star named Mick Jagger who travels to Rio de Janeiro with his wife (played by Jerry Hall, soon to be his real-life wife) and his video director (played by Dennis Hopper) to shoot a video. In a plot development similar to the one in the *Undercover of the Night* video, Jagger is mugged and stranded in the countryside while being given up for dead by the world at large. He makes his way back, aided by a prostitute (played by Rae Dawn Chong), along the way managing to sing all the songs from the album.

Given Jagger's solo singing and acting aspirations, this project may have made some sense to do in late 1984 (when such stars as Michael Jackson and David Bowie were making similar video extravaganzas). But all that came of it was some footage used for music videos of the singles 'Just Another Night' and 'Lucky in Love,' while the full-length version, *Running Out of Luck*, which had a brief theatrical run, didn't appear in video stores until September 26, 1986, much too late to help the album.

Jagger also gave a series of interviews in major publications that appeared simultaneously with the album's release in February, 1985. Speaking to *Rolling Stone* magazine, he denied that the Stones were 'winding down,' saying, 'I don't think so. I mean, we're going into the studio in January, and we're planning a tour for next year. Ronnie said so on MTV! [Laughs] Who am I to say there isn't going to be?'

Jagger told the *New York Times* that a Stones tour was 'quite possible,' and Stones publicist Paul Wasserman told *USA Today* that the Stones would tour the US in the summer of 1985 and the rest of the world in the summer of 1986. The Stones themselves, meanwhile, went into Pathe-Marconi Studios, where they would spend January to April working on their new album. (Eventually, word would leak out of disagreements between Jagger, who had become accustomed to running Stones recording sessions, and Richards who, now drug-free, was asserting himself much more.)

Jagger's first American solo single, 'Just Another Night,' was released on January 23. It reached Number 12 in the US and Number 32 in the UK. The album *She's the Boss* followed, going platinum and reaching Number 13 in the US, Number Six in the UK. The follow-up single was 'Lucky in Love,' which reached Number 38 in the US.

These were relatively disappointing numbers for Jagger, who had made a major effort to establish himself as a solo superstar with the album. But they only caused him to redouble his efforts to achieve solo success.

Bill Wyman and Charlie Watts, meanwhile, had found their own performing outlet and benefit project, as Wyman put together the group Willie and the Poor Boys with several performers from the ARMS shows held to benefit multiple sclerosis. A *Willie and the Poor Boys* album and video were released on April 25.

In other benefit news, on June 29, in preparation for Live Aid, Jagger and David Bowie recorded a special version of Martha and the Vandellas' 'Dancing in the Street' and shot a video as well. The video would be premiered on the Live Aid broadcast, and the single would reach Number Seven in the US and Number One in the UK.

If any more evidence were needed that the Stones were in trouble as a group, Live Aid surely provided it. On July 11, two nights before the event, Richards and

Wood showed up onstage at New York's Lone Star Cafe, where they jammed with guitar legend Lonnie Mack. A tight-lipped Jagger observed the proceedings from the club's upper level, but did not join in. Bob Dylan, also at the club, enlisted Richards and Wood as his backing musicians for Live Aid. On July 13 in Philadelphia, Jagger appeared as a solo artist and with Tina Turner, while the guitarists strummed along with Dylan.

On November 18, Charlie Watts realized a long-held dream when he opened at the jazz club Ronnie Scott's in London with his Big Band, playing swing classics. Jagger and Richards were in the audience. This would be Watts's consuming project for the next couple of years. He would play in halls around England, releasing *Live at Fulham Hall* on November 27, 1986, and even playing selected dates in the US in 1986 and 1987.

*Below:* The reunited Rolling Stones at the press conference held in Grand Central Station in New York to announce their Steel Wheels tour, July 11, 1989.

On December 12, 1985, Ian Stewart became the second of the original Rolling Stones to die, of a heart attack at the age of 47. Stewart had been the group's silent linchpin, and his death would have a major impact in fragmenting the Stones. All five group members attended his funeral on December 20.

At the start of 1986, the Stones began to do interviews to mark the release of the new album, *Dirty Work*. It was at this point that the rifts in the band began to go public, as Jagger made it clear he had no intention of touring and the other band members made it just as clear that a tour was coming. Never one to mince words, Richards said he would cut Jagger's throat if the singer ever toured solo.

The single 'Harlem Shuffle' was released on February 26, followed by *'irty Work* on March 24. The single hit Number Five in the US and Number 13 in the UK, and the album, which went platinum, reached Number Four in the US.

*Dirty Work* included an unusually large number of references to violence and frustration in its lyrics, as can be seen merely in the song titles: 'Had It With You,' 'Back to Zero,' 'Winning Ugly,' 'Fight,' and 'One Hit (to the Body).' The last song was the next single, with a video featuring Jagger and Richards scuffling. Released on May 7, it reached Number 28 in the US and became the first Stones single not to chart in the UK.

With no tour in the offing, the Stones separated in the spring of 1986, apparently without plans to work together again, though no formal break-up was announced. Keith Richards began to plan the 60th birthday party concert he would stage for Chuck Berry in St. Louis in the fall. Prior to this, however, Richards found another legend to work with, taping a version of 'Jumpin' Jack Flash' on July 7-9 in Detroit with Aretha Franklin. The recording would be released in September as the title song for a Whoopi Goldberg film and would reach Number 21.

Jagger, meanwhile, returned to solo work, emerging in late July with the title track to the film *Ruthless People*, a single that got only to Number 51.

On October 16, Richards acted as rhythm guitarist and musical director for the Chuck Berry concert in St. Louis, featuring Eric Clapton, Linda Ronstadt, Robert Cray, Julian Lennon, and Etta James. The film, 'Hail! Hail! Rock 'n' Roll', was released in October, 1987, with a soundtrack album produced by Richards.

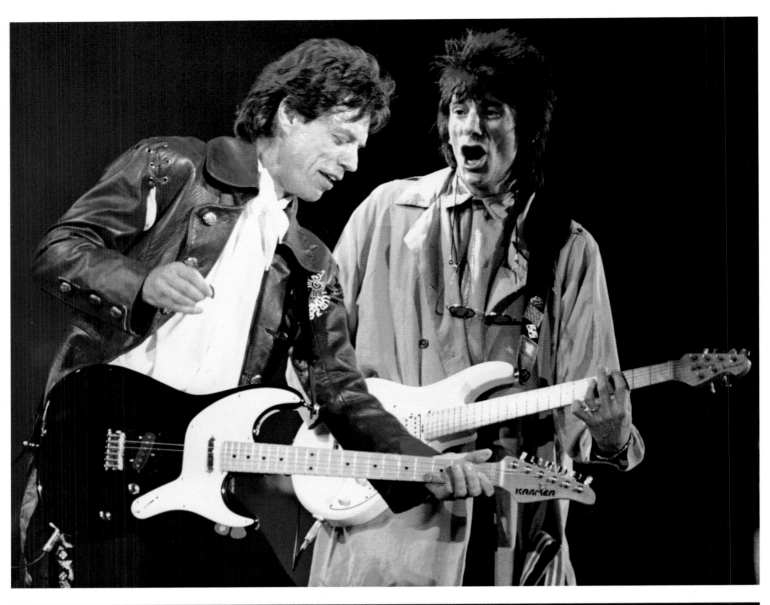

*Left:* Mick Jagger and Ron Wood on guitars at Exhibition Stadium, Toronto, September 3, 1989, before 60,000 fans.

*Below left:* Mick Jagger on the set of his video for 'Say You Will,' a track from his solo album *Primitive Cool*, shot in London, July 27-28, 1987.

*Below:* Forty-six-year-old Mick Jagger in 1989, still looking spry after 25 years of touring the US.

*Previous pages:* The outdoor stage set for the 1989-90 Steel Wheels/Urban Jungle tour.

*Left:* Keith Richards kicks up his heels during the Stones' Urban Jungle tour of Europe, 1990.

*Below left:* A dapper Mick Jagger plays guitar while looking cool on the Urban Jungle tour, 1990.

*Right:* One of the inflatable Honky Tonk Women who accompanied the Stones on tour, 1989-90.

Mick Jagger began recording a second solo album at the start of 1987. Meanwhile, on March 18, Bill Wyman, asked by the UK's 'Music Box' TV channel whether the Stones had broken up, replied, 'It looks that way,' though he added a reunion was possible.

Keith Richards seems to have come to the same conclusion, and in April he began working on his own solo demos. He signed to Virgin Records on July 17 and began formal recording sessions for his debut album in August.

Jagger, meanwhile, finished his second album, and its lead-off single, 'Let's Work,' was released September 1, with the LP, *Primitive Cool*, coming nine days later. Both were major sales disappointments. The single got to only Number 39 (Number 31 in the UK), and the album reached Number 41 (Number 26 in the UK) without even going gold. A second single, 'Throwaway,' lived up to its name by going only to Number 67, and a third single, 'Say You Will,' did not chart.

On March 15, 1988, Jagger launched a two-week solo tour in Japan, during which he performed about 20 Rolling Stones songs. (Keith Richards did not show up to cut his throat, but he did criticize the tour in later interviews.) That seems to have been a signal that Jagger realized his Stones heritage was still much bigger than his solo work. On May 18, Jagger met with the other Stones in London to discuss the group's future.

*Left:* Mick Jagger as he appeared in the role of a bounty hunter in the 1992 movie *Freejack*, his first completed acting job for a feature film in 22 years.

*Below:* The reunited 'Glimmer Twins' onstage during the Steel Wheels/Urban Jungle tour, 1989-90.

*Overleaf:* The Stones at the start of the 1990s, none the worse for wear. Left to right: Keith Richards, Charlie Watts, Mick Jagger, Bill Wyman, Ron Wood.

Richards was taken by surprise. 'As I was finishing the solo album, I got a call from the Stones, saying, 'Band meeting!' about getting together,' he told Stanley Booth in the October, 1989, issue of *Playboy* magazine. Speaking to *Rolling Stone* in August, 1988, Richards said, 'Now [Jagger] wants to put the Stones back together – because there's nowhere else to go.'

Nevertheless, Richards was ready to re-form the group, even though both he and Jagger still had solo work to which they were committed. For Richards, there was his solo album; for Jagger, a Far East tour. Jagger launched his tour, which included Australia and New Zealand, on September 22; it ran through November 5.

Richards's *Talk Is Cheap* was released on September 26. It reached Number 24 in the US and Number 37 in the UK. Richards played a brief concert tour to promote it in the US from November 24 to December 17.

On January 18, 1989, the Rolling Stones were admitted into the Rock and Roll Hall of Fame, by which time plans for their reunion were well advanced. Jagger and Richards flew to Barbados after the ceremony to begin writing songs, then spent February and March recording at Blue Wave Studios there with the rest of the Stones. Sessions continued in April at AIR Studios on the island of Montserrat, and the completed album was mixed at Olympic Studios in London in May – record time for a Stones album.

The Steel Wheels tour was announced at Grand Central Station in New York on July 11. On August 11 came the release of the new album's first single, 'Mixed Emotions,' whose lyrics spoke volumes about the uneasy nature of the reunion. It reached Number Five. The album, *Steel Wheels*, was released on August 29 and went to Number Three.

The tour opened on August 31 in Philadelphia and ran through December 19, concluding with a pay-per-view cable broadcast from Atlantic City, New Jersey. The Stones renamed it 'Urban Jungle' for a set of shows in Europe and the Far East that ran through 1990.

The Stones prepared a live album from the tour, but altered their plans slightly after the invasion of Kuwait by Iraq in August, 1990, to which Mick Jagger responded by writing a song called 'Highwire,' which commented on the West's gunboat diplomacy in the Middle East. The Stones recorded the song and a second studio track, 'Sexdrive,' in December and added the numbers

*Below:* The unflappable
Charlie Watts, still
unimpressed after 30 years,
allowed in 1992 that he
supposed there would be
another Stones album and
tour (ho hum).

*Page 90:* Mick Jagger's third
solo album, *Wandering Spirit*,
went gold in March, 1993.

*Page 91:* Keith Richards saw
1993 in with a concert in New
York broadcast on national
television. His *Main Offender*
album, however, was far from
a hit.

to the album, titled *Flashpoint*, which was released in
April, 1991. 'Highwire,' whose sentiments were much
less enthusiastic than those being expressed by
Americans in the wake of the January military action
dubbed 'Operation Desert Storm,' was released as a
single on March 4 and got to only Number 57. The
album made Number 16.

With this, the Stones had completed their Columbia
Records contract, and they signed a new deal with Virgin Records for three albums said to be valued at
$35-$45 million. The deal also included rights to their
back catalog.

Nineteen ninety-one was a relatively quiet year for the
Stones, though Mick Jagger took his first acting role in
decades, co-starring in a futuristic thriller called *Freejack*, while Keith Richards released an album and video
taken from his 1988 concert tour, reportedly in an effort
to upstage bootleggers.

In 1992, Jagger, Richards, Wood, and Watts all

worked on solo projects. Bill Wyman, reportedly not a
signer to the Virgin Records deal, was said to have quit
the band, though both Jagger and Richards made
efforts to woo him back, which Jagger admitted in
December were unsuccessful. He said the Stones
would seek a new bass player.

Charlie Watts's album featured a jazz quintet playing
a tribute to Charlie Parker. Wood's album, *Slide On
This,* appeared in the fall and promptly disappeared,
and the same fate befell Richards's album, *Main Offender.* Jagger delayed release of his third solo album,
*Wandering Spirit*, until February, 1993.

The Rolling Stones thus concluded 30 years in existence ready to re-organize and play again. Though only
three members remained from the six who originally
formed the group in January, 1963, the Rolling Stones
had managed to hold to their original vision, and as their
two principal members approached the age of 50, the
band's unprecedented career continued.

# Discography

## U.K. RELEASES

**SINGLES**

| Label | Record Number | Title | Year |
|---|---|---|---|
| Decca | F 11675 | Come On/I Want to Be Loved | 1963 |
| Decca | F 11764 | I Wanna Be Your Man/Stoned | 1963 |
| Decca | F 11845 | Not Fade Away/Little By Little | 1964 |
| Decca | F 11934 | It's All Over Now/Good Times, Bad Times | 1964 |
| Decca | F 12014 | Little Red Rooster/Off the Hook | 1964 |
| Decca | F 12104 | The Last Time/Play With Fire | 1965 |
| Decca | F 12220 | (I Can't Get No) Satisfaction/The Spider and the Fly | 1965 |
| Decca | F 12263 | Get Off of My Cloud/The Singer Not the Song | 1965 |
| Decca | F 12331 | 19th Nervous Breakdown/As Tears Go By | 1966 |
| Decca | F 12395 | Paint It Black/Long Long While | 1966 |
| Decca | F 12497 | Have You Seen Your Mother, Baby, Standing in the Shadow?/Who's Driving Your Plane | 1966 |
| Decca | F 12546 | Let's Spend the Night Together/Ruby Tuesday | 1967 |
| Decca | F 12654 | We Love You/Dandelion | 1967 |
| Decca | F 12782 | Jumpin' Jack Flash/Child of the Moon | 1968 |
| Decca | F 12952 | Honky Tonk Women/You Can't Always Get What You Want | 1969 |
| Decca | F 13126 | Little Queenie/Love in Vain | 1970 |
| Rolling Stones | RS 19100 | Brown Sugar/Bitch/Let It Rock | 1971 |
| Decca | F 13195 | Street Fighting Man/Surprise Surprise/Everybody Needs Somebody to Love | 1971 |
| Decca | F 13203 | Street Fighting Man/Surprise Surprise | 1971 |
| R.S. | RS 19103 | Tumbling Dice/Sweet Black Angel | 1972 |
| Decca | F 13404 | Sad Day/You Can't Always Get What You Want | 1973 |
| R.S. | RS 19105 | Angie/Silver Train | 1973 |
| Atlantic | K 19107 | Brown Sugar/Happy/Rocks Off | 1974 |
| R.S. | RS 19114 | It's Only Rock 'N' Roll/Through the Lonely Nights | 1974 |
| Decca | F 13584 | I Don't Know Why/Try a Little Harder | 1975 |
| Decca | F 13597 | Out of Time/Jiving Sister Fanny | 1975 |
| Decca | F 13635 | Honky Tonk Women/Sympathy For the Devil | 1976 |
| R.S. | RS 19121 | Fool to Cry/Crazy Mama | 1976 |
| R.S. | EMI 2802 | Miss You/Far Away Eyes | 1978 |
| R.S. | EMI 2861 | Respectable/When the Whip Comes Down | 1978 |
| R.S. | RSR 105 | Emotional Rescue/Down in the Hole | 1980 |
| R.S. | RSR 106 | She's So Cold/Send It to Me | 1980 |
| R.S. | RSR 108 | Start Me Up/No Use in Crying | 1981 |
| R.S. | RSR 109 | Waiting On a Friend/Little T & A | 1981 |
| R.S. | RSR 110 | Going to a Go Go/Beast of Burden | 1982 |
| R.S. | RSR 111 | Time Is On My Side/Twenty Fight Rock | 1982 |
| R.S. | RSR 113 | Undercover of the Night/All the Way Down | 1983 |
| R.S. | RSR 114 | She Was Hot/I Think I'm Going Mad | 1984 |
| Sugar | 1 | Brown Sugar/Bitch | 1984 |
| CBS | A 6864 | Harlem Shuffle/Had It With You | 1986 |
| CBS | A 7160 | One Hit (to the Body)/Fight | 1986 |
| CBS | 655193-7 | Mixed Emotions/Fancyman Blues | 1989 |
| CBS | 655422-7 | Rock and a Hard Place/Cook Cook Blues | 1989 |

## EPS

| Label | Record Number | Title | Year |
|---|---|---|---|
| Decca | DFE 8560 | The Rolling Stones | 1964 |
| Decca | DFE 8590 | Five by Five | 1964 |
| Decca | DFE 8620 | Got Live If You Want It! | 1965 |

## ALBUMS

| Label | Record Number | Title | Year |
|---|---|---|---|
| Decca | LK 4605 | The Rolling Stones | 1964 |
| Decca | LK 4661 | The Rolling Stones No. 2 | 1965 |
| Decca | SKL 4733 | Out of Our Heads | 1965 |
| Decca | SKL 4786 | Aftermath | 1966 |
| Decca | TXS 101 | Big Hits (High Tide and Green Grass) | 1966 |
| Decca | SKL 4852 | Between the Buttons | 1967 |
| Decca | TXS 103 | Their Satanic Majesties Request | 1967 |
| Decca | SKL 4955 | Beggars Banquet | 1968 |
| Decca | SKL 5019 | Through the Past, Darkly | 1969 |
| Decca | SKL 5025 | Let It Bleed | 1969 |
| Decca | SKL 5065 | Get Yer Ya-Ya's Out! | 1970 |
| Decca | SKL 5084 | Stone Age | 1971 |
| Rolling Stones | COC 59100 | Sticky Fingers | 1971 |
| Decca | SKL 5010 | Gimme Shelter | 1971 |
| Decca | SKL 5098 | Milestones | 1972 |
| R.S. | COC 69100 | Exile on Main Street | 1972 |
| Decca | SKL 5149 | Rock 'N' Rolling Stones | 1972 |
| R.S. | COC 59101 | Goat's Head Soup | 1973 |
| Decca | SKL 5173 | No Stone Unturned | 1973 |
| R.S. | COC 59103 | It's Only Rock 'N' Roll | 1974 |
| R.S. | COC 59104 | Made in the Shade | 1975 |
| Decca | SKL 5212 | Metamorphosis | 1975 |
| Decca | ROST 1/2 | Rolled Gold | 1975 |
| R.S. | COC 59106 | Black and Blue | 1976 |
| R.S. | COC 89101 | Love You Live | 1977 |
| Arcade | ADEP 32 | Get Stoned | 1977 |
| R.S. | CUN 39108 | Some Girls | 1978 |
| R.S. | COC 59107 | Time Waits for No One | 1979 |
| R.S. | CUN 39111 | Emotional Rescue | 1980 |
| Decca | TAB 1 | Solid Rock | 1980 |
| R.S. | CUN 39112 | Sucking in the Seventies | 1981 |
| R.S. | CUNS 39114 | Tattoo You | 1981 |
| Decca | TAB 30 | Slow Rollers | 1981 |
| R.S. | CUN 39115 | Still Life | 1982 |
| K-Tel | NE 1201 | Story of the Stones | 1982 |
| R.S. | CUN 1654361 | Undercover | 1983 |
| CBS | 86321 | Dirty Work | 1986 |
| CBS | 465752-1 | Steel Wheels | 1989 |

# U.S. RELEASES

| | | | |
|---|---|---|---|
| **SINGLES** | | | |
| *Label* | *Record Number* | *Title* | *Year* |
| London | 9657 | Not Fade Away/I Wanna Be Your Man | 1964 |
| London | 9682 | Tell Me/I Just Want to Make Love to You | 1964 |
| London | 9687 | It's All Over Now/Good Times, Bad Times | 1964 |
| London | 9708 | Time Is On My Side/Congratulations | 1964 |
| London | 9725 | Heart of Stone/What a Shame | 1964 |
| London | 9741 | The Last Time/Play With Fire | 1965 |
| London | 9766 | (I Can't Get No) Satisfaction/The Under Assistant West Coast Promotion Man | 1965 |
| London | 9792 | Get Off of My Cloud/I'm Free | 1965 |
| London | 9823 | 19th Nervous Breakdown/Sad Day | 1966 |
| London | 901 | Paint It Black/Stupid Girl | 1966 |
| London | 902 | Mother's Little Helper/Lady Jane | 1966 |
| London | 903 | Have You Seen Your Mother, Baby, Standing in the Shadow?/Who's Driving Your Plane | 1966 |
| London | 904 | Let's Spend the Night Together/Ruby Tuesday | 1967 |
| London | 905 | We Love You/Dandelion | 1967 |
| London | 906 | She's a Rainbow/2000 Light Years From Home | 1967 |
| London | 907 | In Another Land/The Lantern | 1967 |
| London | 908 | Jumpin' Jack Flash/Child of the Moon | 1968 |
| London | 909 | Street Fighting Man/No Expectations | 1968 |
| London | 910 | Honky Tonk Women/You Can't Always Get What You Want | 1969 |
| Rolling Stones | RS 19100 | Brown Sugar/Bitch | 1971 |
| R.S. | RS 19101 | Wild Horses/Sway | 1971 |
| R.S. | RS 19103 | Tumbling Dice/Sweet Black Angel | 1972 |
| R.S. | RS 19104 | Happy/All Down the Line | 1972 |
| R.S. | RS 19105 | Angie/Silver Train | 1973 |
| R.S. | RS 19109 | Doo Doo Doo Doo Doo (Heartbreaker)/Dancing With Mr. D | 1973 |
| R.S. | RS 19301 | It's Only Rock 'N' Roll/Through the Lonely Nights | 1974 |
| R.S. | RS 19302 | Ain't Too Proud to Beg/Dance Little Sister | 1974 |
| ABKCO | 4701 | I Don't Know Why/Try a Little Harder | 1975 |
| ABKCO | 4702 | Out of Time/Jiving Sister Fanny | 1975 |
| R.S. | RS 19304 | Fool to Cry/Hot Stuff | 1976 |
| R.S. | RS 19307 | Miss You/Far Away Eyes | 1978 |
| R.S. | RS 19309 | Beast of Burden/When the Whip Comes Down | 1978 |
| R.S. | RS 19310 | Shattered/Everything Is Turning to Gold | 1978 |
| R.S. | RS 20001 | Emotional Rescue/Down in the Hole | 1980 |
| R.S. | RS 21001 | She's So Cold/Send It to Me | 1980 |
| R.S. | RS 21003 | Start Me Up/No Use in Crying | 1981 |
| R.S. | RS 21004 | Waiting On a Friend/Little T & A | 1981 |
| R.S. | RS 21300 | Neighbors/Hang Fire | 1982 |
| R.S. | RS 21301 | Going to a Go Go/Beast of Burden | 1982 |
| R.S. | RS 7-99978 | Time Is On My Side/Twenty Flight Rock | 1982 |
| R.S. | 7-99813 | Undercover of the Night/All the Way Down | 1983 |
| R.S. | 99788 | She Was Hot/I Think I'm Going Mad | 1984 |
| R.S. | 0-96902 | Too Much Blood/Too Much Blood | 1984 |
| R.S. | 05802 | Harlem Shuffle/Had It With You | 1986 |
| R.S. | 05906 | One Hit (to the Body)/Fight | 1986 |
| R.S. | 69008 | Mixed Emotions/Fancyman Blues | 1989 |
| R.S. | 73057 | Rock and a Hard Place/Cook Cook Blues | 1989 |
| R.S. | 73093 | Almost Hear You Sigh | 1990 |
| R.S. | 73742 | Highwire/2000 Light Years From Home | 1991 |

**ALBUMS**

| Label | Record Number | Title | Year |
|-------|--------------|-------|------|
| London | PS 375 | England's Newest Hitmakers – The Rolling Stones | 1964 |
| London | PS 402 | 12 × 5 | 1964 |
| London | PS 420 | The Rolling Stones, Now! | 1965 |
| London | PS 429 | Out of Our Heads | 1965 |
| London | PS 451 | December's Children | 1965 |
| London | NPS 1 | Big Hits (High Tide and Green Grass) | 1966 |
| London | PS 476 | Aftermath | 1966 |
| London | PS 493 | Got Live If You Want It! | 1966 |
| London | PS 499 | Between the Buttons | 1967 |
| London | PS 509 | Flowers | 1967 |
| London | NPS 2 | Their Satanic Majesties Request | 1967 |
| London | PS 539 | Beggars Banquet | 1968 |
| London | NPS 3 | Through the Past, Darkly | 1969 |
| London | NPS 4 | Let It Bleed | 1969 |
| London | NPS 5 | Get Yer Ya-Ya's Out! | 1970 |
| Rolling Stones | COC 59100 | Sticky Fingers | 1971 |
| London | 2PS 606/607 | Hot Rocks 1964-1971 | 1972 |
| R.S. | COC 2-2900 | Exile on Main Street | 1972 |
| London | 2PS 626/627 | More Hot Rocks | 1972 |
| R.S. | COC 59101 | Goat's Head Soup | 1973 |
| R.S. | COC 79101 | It's Only Rock 'N' Roll | 1974 |
| R.S. | COC 79102 | Made in the Shade | 1975 |
| ABKCO | ANA 1 | Metamorphosis | 1975 |
| R.S. | COC 79104 | Black and Blue | 1976 |
| R.S. | COC 2-9001 | Love You Live | 1977 |
| R.S. | COC 39108 | Some Girls | 1978 |
| R.S. | COC 16015 | Emotional Rescue | 1980 |
| R.S. | COC 16028 | Sucking in the Seventies | 1981 |
| R.S. | COC 16052 | Tattoo You | 1981 |
| R.S. | COC 39113 | Still Life | 1982 |
| R.S. | 90120 | Undercover | 1983 |
| R.S. | 86321 | Dirty Work | 1986 |
| ABKCO | 1218-2 | Singles Collection: The London Years | 1989 |
| R.S. | 45333 | Steel Wheels | 1989 |
| R.S. | 47456 | Flashpoint | 1991 |

# Index